Treehouses Building Guide

Treehouse Planning and How to Build

Copyright © 2022

DEDICATION

Contents

Build a Treehouse

This particular design requires two or three trees (or branches) in close proximity. It was made over the course of several weekends using new, pressure-treated wood for the support structure and floor and an old fence was recycled for the sides. The roof is a camouflage-pattern tarp. It's not weather-proof, but it stays pretty dry inside: a three-season treehouse, but best for summer! It was made with my 4, 6 and 8-year old children in mind, but has been a hit with visitors of all ages.

Step 1: Pick Your Tree(s)

There are definite advantages in using more than one tree for your treehouse - the treehouse can be bigger, and you have to use less bracing. The tree you see here (behind the magnolia!) has a trunk that splits into three at the base, and these trunks splay out somewhat as they grow upwards. At the height of the treehouse - about 9' (2.7 m) off the ground - one pair of trunks are touching, and the other one is about 4' (1.2 m) away. This means the design has been based on one for a closely spaced pair of trees, rather than for a group of three. The tree is a Garry oak, and they don't grow much further north than this (southern Vancouver Island), so they grow pretty slow here. A solid gnarly collection of old trunks, each about 1' in diameter at 9 ft up.

Start by figuring out how high you want the treehouse. 9' is exciting for kids but not scary. You can of course go higher, but you'll have to take more account of tree movement.

Step 2: Design

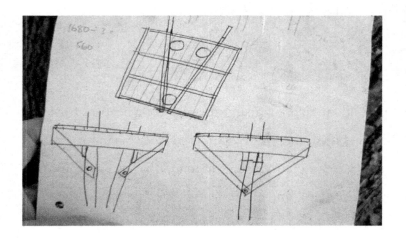

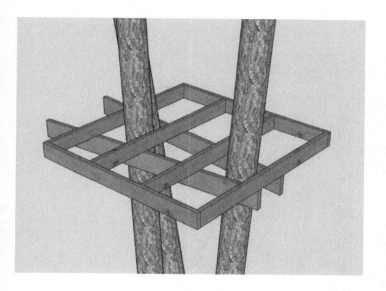

The first photo is of my plan, which was sketched on a cereal box. I read around a lot first, of course. The design changed as I was building it - I didn't end up adding the braces drawn in the bottom left elevation, and I built an entrance platform that I hadn't originally planned. The 3D modelled picture gives a better indication of the layout of the main structure around the trunks.

Step 3: Materials

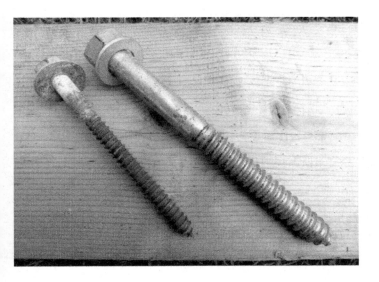

For this treehouse, I bought:

2 8' lengths of 2×8 pressure treated (PT) lumber

6 12' lengths of 1×6 PT decking material

6 8' lengths of 2×6 PT lumber

3 10' lengths of 2×4 PT lumber

3 10" long, 3/4" diameter galvanized lag screws and washers

2 8" long, 3/4" diameter galvanized lag screws and washers

8 galvanized joist hangers

8 galvanized rafter ties

Nails, deck screws, pulley for 1/4" rope

Camouflage tarp

All this cost about $250 from the nearby Home Depot, except for the lag screws and washers which I got online. I also had to buy a really long 5/8" spade bit to bore the holes in the tree. The rest of the materials came from a neighbor's old fence: plentiful amounts of cedar boards and 2×4 lumber. It was used for the sides, so you can just substitute whatever you'd like to make a railing/walls.

The second photo shows the difference between the 1/2" lag screws that held the treehouse up for 4 years, and the 3/4" ones I replaced them with. A **lot** more steel in the big ones!

Step 4: Tools

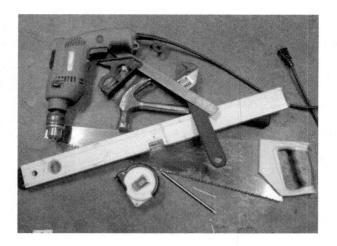

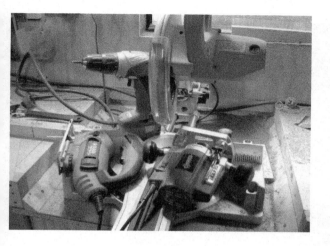

The bare minimum of **hand tools**: hammer, saw, level, square, tape measure, adjustable wrench. **Power tools**: cordless drill, jigsaw

Useful but not critical power tools: miter saw (cutting lumber to length), table saw (ripping lumber), router (rounding edges).

A ladder is important, but even a stepladder would be OK if you installed a ladder/rope ladder/stairs to the treehouse early in the build.

Step 5: Mount the Main Supports

Get a strip of light wood and nail one end to one of your trees at a height about 1 ft lower than you want the floor of your treehouse (to save a future concussion, it should also be at **least** 1 ft higher than your head!). Get it perfectly horizontal with the help of a level and nail the other end to the other tree. Drill 5/8" holes straight into the tree just above the strip of wood. Do the same on the other side of the trees, this time taking the extra precaution of first ensuring the new strip is not only horizontal but also level with the strip on the other side of the tree.

Now, take down the strips and measure the exact distance between the holes. Subtract this distance from 6' (not 8', unless you don't want the entrance platform), halve the remainder, and make a mark this distance away from one end of your 2×8. Drill a 3/4" hole in the middle of the board. Make another mark using the between-the-holes measurement . Now drill two 3/4" holes, each 1-2" either side of your mark and both in the middle of the board. Get a jigsaw and make two cuts between the holes to make a 2-4" long slot. Repeat for the other side of the tree. The slot allows the trees to move without tearing your treehouse apart - the more your trees move, the longer the slot ought to be (note that the slots I cut are only about 2" long, but these trees don't move perceptibly at the height of the treehouse, even in a strong wind. If your trees move appreciably, and/or if you're planning to build higher up, use a sliding beam support).

Drive the screws through the holes in the boards and into the tree with a wrench. Use washers, and don't bolt hard against the tree. The space you're giving it to grow is the gap between the support and the tree. The longer you want your treehouse to last, the further you should perch the support away - and the more substantial your lag screws ought to be! I know my tree grew only by about 1/4"-1/2" in diameter over 4 years, but most trees grow faster than this. When I rebuilt the treehouse with 3/4" lag bolts, I gave it about 1/2" to grow on either side. I used 10" bolts for the trees with one bolt in them, and 8" bolts for the tree with two bolts in it.

Step 6: Lay Out the Platform

Because the decking came in 12' long boards, I made the treehouse 6' long. So you need to cut the decking in half, and lay it out. Leave a small gap between boards for drainage. Cut two of your 2×6 boards the same length as the decking, and the other four to the width of your decking less the thickness of two of the 2×6's (which will be more like 1 1/2" each).

Step 7: Build the Platform

Using 3" deck screws, attach the four 2×6's perpendicularly to one of the other 2×6's. Make sure they're spaced so that when you put it up in the tree, the perpendicular joists will miss the tree! With someone's help, put the contraption up in the tree, center it, and tie it down.

Screw the other 2×6 to the other end of the platform, and check that it is centered and square. For squareness, measure the diagonals and ensure they are the same.

Step 8: Attach Platform to Supports

Now use the rafter ties to attach your platform to the 2×8s that you screwed to the tree (if the angles between joists are not exactly 90°, no problem, just hammer the rafter tie flat against each joist as you're nailing). Add the joist hangers. Use galvanized nails to attach these, not screws.

Step 9: Brace the Platform

As it is, the platform will wobble dangerously. Add diagonal bracing made of 2×4, and use a single long lag screw to attach both of these to the tree. It's easiest to just cut the 45 degree angle in the 2×4 first. Use an 10" lag screw here to make up for the fact that you're going through 2 thicknesses of lumber.

Note that I just used one set of braces on the single tree, because the other end had two trees and the wobble seemed insignificant. You'll need two sets for sure if you have just a pair of trees.

Step 10: Hang a Pulley

A pulley is great fun for kids, but it's helpful for hauling tools etc. up to the deck. Put one in now, and hang a basket from it. A climbing carabiner at the end of the rope is perfect for quick disconnects.

If you don't have a suitably overhanging trunk or branch, you'll just have to make one. Lag screw a 2×4 (or similar) between the two trees well above the deck (cut a long slot to accommodate movement, because you're higher up the tree), and have it protrude far enough to

24

hang the pulley from. Bonus: you'll also have a ridgepole for your roof!

Step 11: Lay the Deck

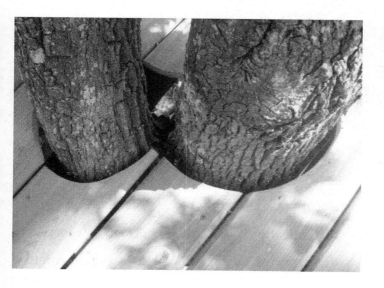

Get up on your platform and screw down the deck. The only tricky thing here is cutting around the trunks. Use sheets of newspaper to make templates so you can cut out the holes reasonably accurately. Be sure to leave space for tree growth and movement.

Step 12: Add an Entranceway

OK, so far the build has been very conventional - all the books on treehouses will tell you how to get this far. One of my favorite bits was the following minor innovation. The two big supports poke out far past the platform, and you can use one set of these to make a slightly lower level to use as an entry. Make a small deck between the tops of the supports to about 2' out, then build diagonally back to the corner of the treehouse. Add verticals. The pictures tell the story here. I just used offcuts - with any luck you'll be able to do the same.

Step 13: Railing

I had lots of 2×4 from the recycled fence, so I used two 40" lengths at each corner as uprights. I screwed them to each other first then nailed them to the platform. The handrail was also 2×4, laid flat, and screwed straight down into the uprights. I mitered the corners, and screwed the handrails to each other through the miter.

Use whatever you like to fill in under the railing - rope, plywood, whatever. Kids probably shouldn't be able to slip through, though. I had lots of nicely weathered cedar boards which I just nailed up. I used strips of 1×1 to hold them in place either side under the railing. The only tricky bit was the angled bit leading down to the platform - a bit of trial and error here, because it is non-trivial to line up the railing with the sides of the platform.

Step 14: Ladder

The plan was to use a rope ladder to get up, but my 4 year old struggled with the transition to the platform, even though he could climb it just fine. So we vetoed it, even after making a pretty nice ladder. I leaned a couple of 2×4s against the entryway, cut the angle, and nailed on two thicknesses of cedar board all the way up. The plan was to put climbing holds up a wall, but I ended up just cutting foot/handholds instead. I'd like to say this was free, but I wore out a big spade bit cutting the holes - it got too hot, and bent. This job was easy if a little time consuming to do - mark and drill two big holes, mark a line between them at the bottom and an arc at the top (I used a plastic bucket) and cut out with a jigsaw. This had really rough edges, so I rounded them off with my little router. That worked great, so I went around quite a few other edges on the treehouse with it. Smooth!

Step 15: Roof

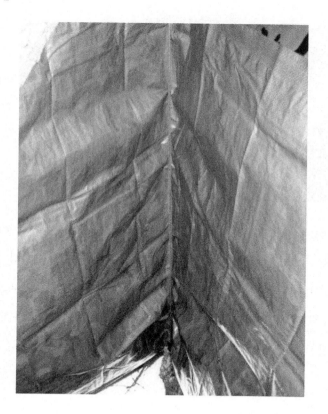

I just strung a bungee cord between two hooks I put into the trees at about 7' above the deck, and slung a tarp over. This looked good, but in actual fact it made the roof too low at the sides. I have a compound mitre saw, so I cut four outriggers, screwed them to the uprights, and gave the treehouse roof a decent overhang.

Step 16: Enjoy!

The treehouse is a great little (36 sq. ft.) haven for the kids; they love it and so do all their friends.

Update May 2013: I'm happy to report the treehouse is four years old now, it's suffered no damage from windstorms, snow, or tree growth (yet...), the trees are healthy, and it still gets lots of use. We've made a few updates over the years, adding a pirate's treasure chest, a swing, a braided climbing rope, a BEWARE sign we use out front at Halloween, and it's well-equipped with Nerf guns & water pistols. It's just big enough for two single air mattresses, so it's fun to sleep out in, too.

Update October 2013: Growth got to the point that I took the treehouse down for safety reasons. The tree started to open some joints, cracks had appeared in the main structural supports, and the washers were embedded in the wood. Amazingly enough, I was able to remove ALL of the lag screws, so when I rebuild I can reuse the same holes (and all the wood except for the 2×8s).

Update July 2014: The treehouse has been fully rebuilt. The instructable has been rewritten to reflect the rebuilding process, and there are a mixture of old and new photos throughout. Main changes: walls no longer have gaps, entry deck has been embiggened, and longer, heavier duty lag screws were used to give more room for the tree to grow. I anticipate it lasting at least another 5 years before taking it down again (probably permanently, as my kids will have outgrown it).

Step 17: Removing the Treehouse

10 years on from the original build and 5 years since the rebuild, my kids had outgrown the treefort. So we took it down - a pretty straightforward demolition. The tree has been completely unaffected by having a structure in it for a decade, and the bolts all came out with a bit of encouragement (I did have to buy a bigger wrench!). To prevent bugs setting up a home in the tree and potentially causing rot, I whittled some oak branch offcuts to the size of the holes and hammered them into the tree. I then cut them off flush.

It felt a bit like the end of an era taking it down, but it has had a great run and we got a lot of enjoyment out of it.

Preparing to Build Your Treehouse

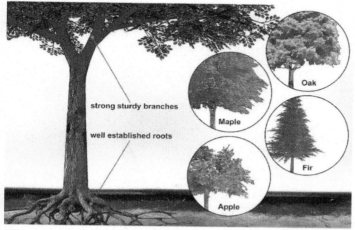

Choose the right tree. The health of the tree you select is absolutely crucial for building a foundation for your treehouse. If the tree is too old or too young, you won't have the support you need for your treehouse and you will be putting yourself and anyone else who goes into the treehouse in great danger. Your tree should be sturdy, healthy, mature, and living. Ideal trees for treehouse include oak, maple, fir, and apple. It's a good idea to have an arborist inspect your tree before you start building. An ideal tree has the following qualities.

A strong, sturdy trunk and branches.

Roots that are deep and well-established!

41

No evidence of disease or parasites that could weaken the tree.

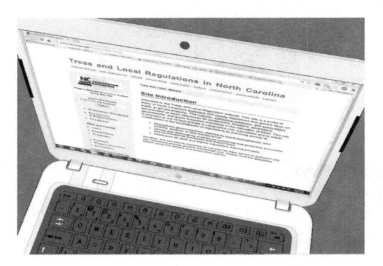

Check with your local planning department. Take the time to learn about local regulations or ordinances that may be relevant to your treehouse project, such as height restrictions. You may even need a permit to build. If you have protected trees on your property, there may be restrictions on building in them

Talk to your neighbors. As a courtesy, it's a good idea to speak with your neighbors and let them know your plans. If your treehouse will be visible from or overlook a neighbor's property, they will be glad you're taking their opinion into consideration. This simple step can head off future complaints and even potential lawsuits. Though your neighbors will most likely comply, this will help make them more amenable to your project.

Talk to your insurance agent. Make a quick call to your insurance agent to make sure that a treehouse is covered under your homeowner's policy. If it's not, then any potential damage that is caused by the treehouse won't be covered by your insurance.

Making a Detailed Plan

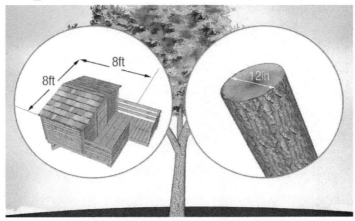

Choose your tree. If you're building a treehouse in your backyard, then you may only have so many trees to choose from. Once you have chosen a healthy tree, you can start thinking about the design of the house that can go on it; or you can take the opposite route and think of the design first, and then make sure that you have a fitting tree. Here are some things you keep in mind as you choose the tree for your treehouse:

For a standard 8'x8' treehouse, choose a tree with a trunk at least 12" in diameter.

To calculate your tree's diameter, measure its circumference by wrapping a string or measuring tape around the trunk at the point where you want the treehouse to sit. Divide that number by pi (3.14) to get the diameter.

Choose your design. It's important to have a firm idea of the design of your dream treehouse before you hammer in the first nail. You can find treehouse designs online,[3] or if you're knowledgeable about building, you can create your own. You need to make accurate measurements to ensure that your design works with the tree you've selected.

You may find it helpful to make a small cardboard model of your tree and treehouse to identify any potential issue areas.

In creating your design, don't forget to plan for tree growth. Allow ample space around the trunk of the tree for the tree to grow. It's worth doing some research on your specific tree species to determine its growth rate.

Decide on your support method. There are several ways to support your treehouse. Whatever method you choose, it's important to remember that trees move with the wind. Sliding joists or brackets are essential to make sure your tree and treehouse are not damaged by winds. Here are the three main support methods for your tree:[4]

The post method. This method involves sinking support posts into the ground close to the tree, rather than attaching anything to the tree itself. It is the least damaging to the tree.

The bolt method. Bolting the support beams or floor platform directly into the tree is the most traditional method of supporting a treehouse. However, this method is the most damaging to the tree. You can minimize the damage by using proper materials.

The suspension method. In this method, you would suspend the treehouse from strong, high branches using cables, rope or chains. This method will not work for every design, and it is not ideal for treehouses that are meant to carry any significant weight.

Decide on your access method. Before you build your treehouse, you'll need to decide on a method of access, such as a ladder, which easily allows a person to enter the treehouse. Your method should be safe and sturdy, so this rules out the traditional treehouse ladder, which is made up of boards nailed to a tree trunk. Here are some safer methods of access for a treehouse:

The standard ladder. You can purchase or build an ordinary ladder for climbing into your treehouse. A ladder made for bunk or loft beds can work as well.

The rope ladder. This is a ladder made of rope and short boards, which is hung from the treehouse platform.

The staircase. A small staircase is the safest access method if it's compatible with your vision of a treehouse. If you choose this method, make sure to build a railing for safety.

Figure out what you'll do with branches that interfere with your treehouse. How will you build around pesky branches? Will you cut them off, or incorporate them into the plans of the treehouse? If you decide to incorporate branches into the treehouse, will you build around them or frame them in a window? Ask yourself these questions before you start building. That way, your treehouse will reflect the care and preparation of its builder when finished.

Building and Securing a Platform

Keep safety in mind. Before you begin to build your treehouse, you should remember to keep safety in mind.[5] Falling out is one of the biggest hazards of a treehouse. There are a few precautions you can take to make sure that everyone who is building the treehouse stays safe.

Don't build too high. Building your treehouse too high could be dangerous. If your treehouse is going to be used mostly by children, the platform should not be any higher than 6–8 feet (1.8–2.4 m).

Construct a safe railing. The point of your railing, of course, is to make sure that the treehouse occupants don't fall out. Make sure the railing around your platform is at least 36" high, with balusters no more than 4" apart.

Cushion a fall. Surround the area below the treehouse with a soft natural material like wood mulch. This won't entirely prevent injury, but it will provide some cushioning for a fall.

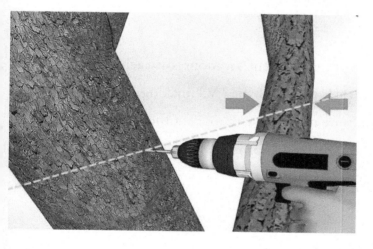

Find a sturdy tree where two branches separate into a "V" shape. You'll use this tree in order to rig up your treehouse. The "V" shape will add extra strength and support, providing an anchor point at four places instead of only at two.

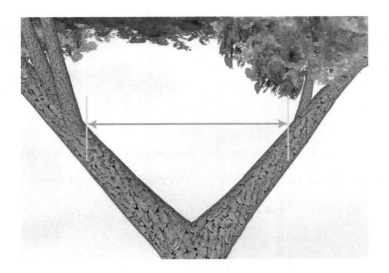

Pre-drill the tree at four different locations, on each side of the "V". Drill a 3/8" into each prong of the "V," making sure that the holes are all level. If they are not level with one another, the structure could be slanted and the support compromised.

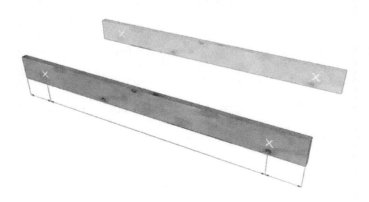

Measure the distance between the holes at each side of the "V". Depending on the tree, the holes may be spaced farther or shorter apart.

Subtract the measurement from 10', halve the rest, and mark the distance from one end of the 2x10. Make a mark at the other end using the original measurement between the two holes in the tree. This will ensure that the 2x10s will be perfectly centered and bear equal weight when you hoist them onto the "V".

Create a 4" slot at each mark on both 2x10s. This is so that the trees can sway in the wind and move without damaging the structural integrity of the treehouse. Do this by drilling two 5/8" holes, each 2" to either side of your mark. Then use a jigsaw to cut between the holes, creating a 4" slot, with your mark completely centered.

Now when the tree sways in the wind, the platform actually moves a bit to accommodate the swaying. If the platform were simply bolted onto the tree, it would move along with the tree. This is not good for the platform, as it could gradually or suddenly be pushed in different directions and begin cracking.

Mount two main supports to the tree at the appropriate height. Choose two sturdy pieces of 2x10 (2x12 will do, too) and place them flush against your tree. Drive four 6" or 8" long, 5/8" diameter galvanized lag screws into the four 4" slots of the 2x10 using a wrench. Place washers in between the screw and the wood board. Repeat with the other board on the opposite side of the trunk, making sure both boards are at equal height and flush with one another.

Pre-drill both the tree and the 2x10s for an easier time installing the screws, and to minimize cracking in your boards.

Undercut both supports at each for an aesthetic finish. Of course, do this before mounting the supports to the trunk with your screws.

Consider doubling up each support with another 2x10 for added strength. In effect use two 2x10s on each side of the trunk, flush against one another. This allows the supports to bear more weight. If you do decide to double up on your supports, use bigger lag screws (at least 8" long and 1" diameter).

Place four 2x6s, evenly spaced, perpendicular across the main supports. Instead of placing them flat across the main supports, place them up on their side so they stick up two feet into the air. Secure them with 3" deck screws.

Attach two 2x6s to the 2x6s nailed into place above. Lay each 2x6 flush across the four ends of the 2x6s and nail them into place. Your platform should now be a square attached to the main supports. Check that your 2x6s are centered and square.

Attach the platform to the main supports with rafter ties. Use 8 galvanized rafter ties to attach all four of the perpendicular 2x6s to the main supports.

Image titled Build a Treehouse Step 20

11

Attach the middle of the platform to the sides of the platform with joist hangers. Use 8 galvanized joist hangers to attach the ends of the perpendicular 2x6s to the abutting 2x6s.

Brace the platform with 2x4s. As it stands now, the platform is still a bit wobbly. In order to make the platform more sturdy, you'll need to add at least two braces. These will be attached to a lower portion of the tree and then again on both edges of the platform.

Cut a 45-degree angle out of the top ends on each 2x4. This is so that you can attach the 2x4 to the inside of the platform.

Form a "V" with your 2x4 so that they overlap at a straight part of the tree but also cleanly abut onto the inside of the platform.

Attach the top of the bracing to the platform from the bottom and on the inside. Make sure both are completely flush before you drive nails into them.

Drive an 8" lag screw through the overlapping 2x4s at a sturdy point on the tree. Use a washer between the 2x4s and the lag screw for the best results.

Laying the Deck and Railing

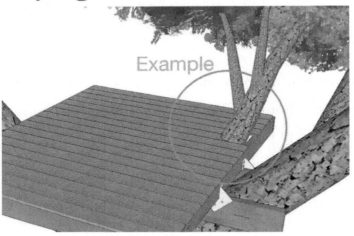

Figure out where you'll need to cut around to fit the trees through your floorboards. Make a measurement of where the trees come through the flooring and cut around the trunks with a jigsaw, leaving 1" to 2" around.

Screw in two screws at each board end with at least 4" deck screws. Once your deck boards have been cut to accommodate the trunks of your tree, it's time to screw them into place. Use a ladder to hoist yourself up onto the platform and start screwing down with a drill. Leave a slight 1/4" or 1/2" distance between each floorboard.

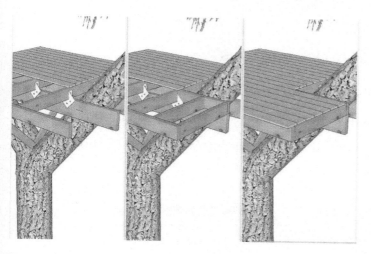

Make an entrance from the main supports that travel past the platform. Add covering and verticals to the platform to make a rectangle. Now an awkward part that formerly jutted out of the platform has been turned into a handy-dandy entrance.

Use two 2x4s at each corner to start making uprights for the railing. Nail the two 2x4 (they should be at least 4 feet high) together, and then screw them to the platform at each corner.

Attach handrails to the uprights. Use 2x4s as well, and if you want, mitre the edges of the handrails. Then, nail them down to the uprights. Next, screw the handrails into one another through their mitered corners.

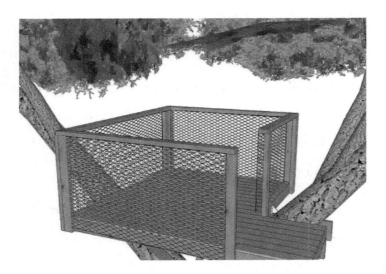

Attach the siding to the bottom of the platform and the bottom

of the handrails. Nail any available woods — planks or plywood work fine — flush into the bottom of the platform. Then nail them into the railing at the top so that they form an effective fence.

- Use whatever you want for siding. You can successfully use meshed-together rope if you want, as long as little kiddies cannot slip through. Safety should be the first priority, especially when you're dealing with small children.

Made in the USA
Middletown, DE
09 October 2023